MY THERAPIST TOLD ME TO JOURNAL

MY THERAPIST TOLD ME TO JOURNAL

A Creative Mental Health Workbook

HOLLY CHISHOLM
Creator of Just Peachy Comics

Skyhorse Publishing

Copyright © 2020 by Holly Chisholm
Special thanks to the American Foundation for Suicide Prevention for content review
and guidance on safe messaging.

**American
Foundation
for Suicide
Prevention**

Skyhorse Publishing books may be purchased in bulk at special discounts for
sales promotion, corporate gifts, fund-raising, or educational purposes. Special
editions can also be created to specifications. For details, contact the Special Sales
Department, Skyhorse Publishing, 307 West 36th Street, 11th Floor, New York, NY
10018 or info@skyhorsepublishing.com.

Skyhorse® and Skyhorse Publishing® are registered trademarks of Skyhorse
Publishing, Inc.®, a Delaware corporation.

Visit our website at www.skyhorsepublishing.com.

10 9 8 7

Library of Congress Cataloging-in-Publication Data

Names: Chisholm, Holly, author.
Title: My therapist told me to journal : a creative mental health workbook
 / Holly Chisholm.
Description: New York, NY : Skyhorse Publishing, [2020] | Identifiers: LCCN
2020022700 | ISBN 9781510761124 (hardcover)
Subjects: LCSH: Diaries--Authorship--Therapeutic use.
Classification: LCC RC489.D5 C45 2020 | DDC 616.89/1663--dc23
LC record available at https://lccn.loc.gov/2020022700

Cover design by Daniel Brount
Cover illustrations by Holly Chisholm

ISBN: 978-1-5107-6112-4

Printed in China

Contents

MY THERAPIST TOLD ME TO JOURNAL

hello!

It's nice to meet you! I am guessing that if you picked this book up, you probably also have a therapist who told you to journal. I am also guessing, if you are anything like me, you might be avoiding journaling for a variety of reasons. Maybe you don't know where to start, or are refusing to journal out of spite, or maybe you just feel lazy and would rather do something else. Don't worry, I can relate. This book, and many others, are the *product* of spite and laziness, which aren't always bad things.

I was diagnosed with depression and ADHD in the winter of 2016 after going through a terrible breakup and moving to Los Angeles. My new (and very first ever) therapist told me that I should keep a journal so I could keep track of how I was feeling. This seems like a simple enough task, but here's the thing: I hate journaling. Like, a lot. Hear me out.

Whenever I think of journaling, here's what pops in my head: A teenage girl (me) with a pink flowery notebook complaining to the universe about petty shit. I have filled a few notebooks with whining, and every attempt to go back and read my younger self's laments made me cringe with embarrassment.

Usually, I would write about how "Josh didn't even LOOK at me today," or how "I didn't get to go out to ice cream with Jessica, so my LIFE IS RUINED."

The thought of looking back compared with my current suffering and realizing I was just being whiny and angsty about everything was too much for me to bear. Also, my current situation seemed to crave more *gravitas* than a notebook with unicorns on it could provide.

Another issue: I always manage to turn journaling into a full-time job. I've gone through what I like to call "self-help guru" phases, where I try to organize my life by logging every little thing I have to do in lists. I've meticulously tracked everything from how many glasses of water I have, to how many times I have a bowel movement. It's gross. It's embarrassing. And worst of all, it's not even helpful. These frantic attempts to completely organize my life to that of a C-level Toyota executive always backfire horribly and quickly. Turns out, it takes a long time to set up all those little lists. Every time I would "miss" a task on my calendar, I would mercilessly beat myself up for not instantly transforming into a perfect being overnight. *Oh, you didn't wake up at 4:30 a.m., go for a five-mile jog, meditate, cook a healthy vegan meal, and then work on your autobiographical novel? YOU ARE A DISGRACE AND GARBAGE, the list says so!*

It sucks because I really, really want to be a list person, but every time I try to be, I end up hating myself more. Also, this kind of journaling can be very discouraging when you are depressed because some days you don't want to do *anything*. A giant to-do list will loom over you and make you feel like a total loser (which isn't right, but feels true sometimes if you're suffering from a mental illness). To-do lists are for the dogs.

I think it's important here to bring up bullet journaling, which tricked me into thinking it was a more "creative" form of journaling. I was lured in by all the fancy markers and accessories you need to complete a perfect bullet journal. *Do not be fooled.* For me, this was by far the worst form of journaling because I spent at least five times longer designing my title page then I did actually writing in my notebook. Bullet journaling could be useful for people with unlimited time and twenty tons of washi tape, but I have neither of those things. So here we are at the beginning of this journal, which I began to create as a very long and complicated way to avoid having to do my therapy homework. Basically, I wanted to create something for people who hate writing and list-keeping, but still want to show their therapist that they are doing *some*thing. This book is also for people who don't have time to become a seventeenth-century calligraphist. Seriously, bullet-journal people, how do you do it?

I hope this journal works for you . . . and your therapist.

What to expect in this book:

Some silly things

Some serious things

Some advice
(which worked for me, but you don't have to take)

Some exercises
(that you don't HAVE to do if you don't want to)

Some resources
(for if you need a little help)

Stickers.
Oh yeah, baby.

nice.

wow

Emergency Pages

Are you having a really, really, really bad day? Here's your emotional emergency bible that addresses some "worst day ever" scenarios.

Everything Sucks

if you are
FEELING DEPRESSED

(If you are feeling suicidal, please turn the page.)

Everyone feels depressed from time to time, but if you are noticing you have been in a low mood for more than two weeks, you could have clinical depression. Sometimes depression will go away naturally with time and care. However, in some cases, you may need to see a doctor or psychiatrist to help you manage symptoms and address the root of what is causing the depression. Whatever the case, here are some steps you can take to begin to feel better!

Phone a friend (who is a good listener).

Sometimes we need a listening ear to remind us that our thoughts might be biased and that we are being too hard on ourselves. However, it is crucial not to just expect our friends to be free therapists for us all the time. Be sure that for as much as you vent, you are also available to listen and provide support right back.

Get outside.

Sunshine is essential to how humans make happy/good feelings in their brains. This sounds trivial, but a 10- to 20-minute walk out in nature can be a lifesaver if you are feeling down.

Pet a puppy.

Seriously though, contact with animals has been clinically proven to help lower blood pressure and increase overall wellbeing. Plus, they are so darn cute. My dog, Bubbles, and cat, Cosmo, have been essential in improving my mental health.

Take care of your basic needs.

Sometimes when we are depressed, we forget to take care of ourselves, and it can make us feel worse. If you can, do something right now that you know you have forgotten to do, like take a shower or brush your teeth. Something that helps me feel better is dressing up and doing my makeup as if I was "going out" even if all I really end up doing is crying on the floor at home.

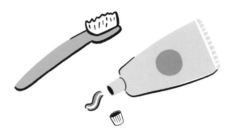

Cut down on the drinking.

Alcohol is a depressant, and can stay in your system for up to seven days. So, lay off the sad juice for a while! Just give it a try and see how you end up feeling.

Try the silly voice trick.

Sometimes my mind can be exceedingly cruel and tell me things that just simply are not true. Whenever this happens, I try to catch my mind and repeat back some of the mean stuff it is saying in a silly voice (I'M a DuMb FaILuRe. I'm NoT gOoD eNoUgH). This method helps me detach from my thoughts and recognize them for what they are: unhelpful.

if you are
FEELING SUICIDAL

Call, text, or message a suicide hotline.

There are lots of different options for getting help. You don't even have to call if you don't want to. Here is a list of some great 24-hour resources in case you want someone to talk to:

Call
National Suicide Prevention Lifeline
1-800-273-8255

Online Chat
National Suicide Prevention Lifeline
suicidepreventionlifeline.org/chat/

Text
Crisis Text Line
Text HOME to 741741

Consider checking yourself into a care facility.

If you think you are at immediate risk of attempting suicide or harming yourself, please consider calling 911 or checking yourself into a mental health facility. You can also call the National Suicide Prevention Lifeline at 1-800-273-TALK or text TALK to 741741. If you don't think you can do it, ask someone else like a close friend, family member, or therapist to help you. Please know that they want to help and that you are not a burden for attempting to stay alive.

Call your therapist (or reach out to one if you don't have one).

If your therapist is available, they can help walk you through your suicidal thoughts and make sure that you get the care you need. Talk to your therapist about developing a safety plan for when you feel this way. If you don't have a therapist, it's a good time to find one. Have a friend help you make that call if you are scared.

Call a trusted friend or family member, even if you don't want to.

It can be challenging to reach out when we are in need because our depression will often tell us that we are a burden to others. This is simply a lie. Our brain often distorts our normal thinking processes when we are depressed, telling us unhelpful things over and over. Here's a way to reframe it: if a friend of yours was going through a tough time, would you want them to reach out to you to ask for help?

Find your "why."

Friedrich Nietzsche said, "He who has a *why* to live for can bear almost any *how*." If you can think of even one reason why you might be here or have a purpose, then write it down in the space below, and you can come back to it if you are feeling suicidal again. Do you have siblings or parents or friends who you can make smile? Do you have a plant that needs you to water it to stay alive? Is there a place you've never been to that you could still live to see one day? Could the pain you are going through now one day be an inspirational story for others who are going through a similar situation? Whatever your reason, I am happy you are still here. If you need help finding out your "why," there are additional helpful exercises on page 48.

My "Why":

if you are
FEELING ANXIOUS

 Anxiety can be a real bastard. Nausea, sweating, tense shoulders, labored breathing, and panic tears make anxiety one of the more physically noticeable mental health problems. Not to worry, 'cause we can beat this B together.

Deep breaths are the anxiety killer.

Panic attacks are caused by a lack of oxygen to the brain, which releases a lot of adrenaline, overwhelming your system and causing a panic attack. Basically, your body thinks it is suffocating, so it freaks out. This can be solved by taking deep, calming breaths. Breathe in for 8 seconds, hold for 6, and breathe out for 8 again. Repeat for as long as you need to avoid a panic attack. You can also breathe into a pillow or paper bag to help slow down your breaths.

Go for a walk.

When you are feeling anxious, your body jumps to the "fight or flight" mode. Since it's probably not worth it to suplex your coworker to release anxiety, try going for a brisk walk instead. Your brain just really wants to burn off some of that nervous energy, and you can do that with some light exercise. If you can't leave the situation you are in, try doing calf raises or shaking your legs a bit.

Detach from your thoughts.
Sometimes in panic mode, I will desperately cling to one idea, like how my cat Cosmo clings to me when I try to give him a bath. Try to identify the thought that's causing you anxiety and detach from it. Picture the thought as words on a computer screen. Change the font of the words. Now the color. Put the words on a silly background. This exercise sounds weird, but it can help you realize that your thoughts are just words and that you can decide if they are helpful to you or not.

Listen to calming music.
I always forget that music can completely change my mood. It's good to have a playlist of songs ready for when you are feeling stressed. I personally have a calming playlist full of piano and video game music for such occasions.

Avoid caffeine and other stimulants.
Too much caffeine can make your anxiety waaay worse. This also goes for nicotine. Try to limit yourself to no more than two cups of joe a day, and consider quitting nicotine altogether if you have bad anxiety.

Change or accept the anxiety.
If you know there is something directly causing your anxiety, and you can change it, do it! If it's something you can't change, then see if you can sit with the discomfort for a while. Often we try to avoid unpleasant feelings instead of feeling them, which only makes them worse.

if you are
FEELING ANGRY
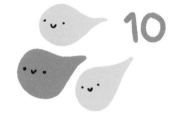

If you are feeling angry and decided to read this book for help, then congratulations because you are already much more self-controlled than I am!

Take 10 deep breaths before you say anything.

You are allowed to express your anger, but it is essential to do it in a way that is healthy and not purely out of rage. Taking several deep breaths before you say something you know you will regret later is a great way to become aware of your anger and will help calm you down.

Take a "time out."

Time outs aren't just for kids. Sometimes when I am angry, I realize I need to remove myself from the person or thing and just take a break for a second. Often if I come back to a frustrating problem fifteen minutes later, then I can tackle the problem with more control.

Go for a walk or jog.

When your brain enters "fight" mode, you produce a lot of adrenaline, and your body needs somewhere to put all that energy. It can be productive to go for a quick jog to release some of the energy that is building up.

FIGHT ME, BRO!

CHILL OUT. LET'S GO FOR A WALK

Write it out.

Write out what is making you frustrated or angry. Often times, we want to just scream our frustrations at a person, but that's a crappy way to maturely express what we are feeling. Writing out your thoughts can help you understand WHY you are upset and help you vent. This can be helpful when you face a frustrating person or situation again. Plus, you can call someone a slack-jawed jabroney without any blowback, which is nice.

fuck you

Helpful

Not helpful

Ask, "Is this helpful?"

A lot of times, our anger comes from injustices that are done to other people or to us. Often we only care about the fact that "I am right, and they are wrong." People can become addicted to this feeling of righteous fury (See: the politics side of Twitter). An important question to ask yourself is, "Even if I am right, is getting angry about the situation actually helpful to me right now?" A lot of times, anger will only end up hurting you, and it is good to know the difference between helpful and unhelpful anger.

Take an anger management class or join a therapy group.

If you have a lot of repeated anger issues or are afraid you might hurt yourself or someone else, then you may need professional help. Remember, anger is a natural human emotion, and there is no shame in seeking help for learning how to control it in a healthy way.

if you are
SUFFERING FROM CHRONIC ILLNESS OR PAIN

If you are suffering from chronic illness or pain, it can often feel very isolating. Here are a few tips to help.

Find a support group.
Many people are going through what you are experiencing or something similar. Sharing those experiences in a group with others who truly understand can be incredibly healing.

Take control of your treatment.
Doctors are often willing to work with you to find the best treatment options. If you want to try something new or current treatment isn't working as well as you hoped, do not be afraid to try something different. This can also help you feel more empowered.

Acceptance through mindfulness.

Our suffering can tend to seem cruel and unfair. It is helpful to practice mindfulness to help us come to terms with the things we cannot change. When we are mindful, we don't view experiences as "good" or "bad," and instead accept them just as they are.

Find your "why."

When suffering seems unnecessary, it is vital to find a "why" unique to your situation. Has your illness made you more sympathetic to the plight of others? Can your story inspire other people in the same situation? Have you grown closer to the people around you? It can be very empowering to realize what is unique about you and understanding why it is that you are here.

if you are
FEELING GRIEF

There is no way to "properly" grieve. It can often be a messy, confusing, and painful process. It is also one of the things that makes us human and help us appreciate the things and people we love. Any sort of significant life change can cause grief, and you don't have to justify it to anyone.

Be patient with yourself.
Grief looks different for everyone, and you don't need to judge yourself harshly for acting strangely or feeling out of control. It's okay to cry "randomly," or cry a lot, or not cry at all. You probably will feel a bit unstable and strange, and that's okay.

Find support.
If people reach out to you during this time, it can be easy to want to isolate and turn away from help. If you can, please let people in and lean on them for support. You don't have to be strong for anyone at this time, and keeping your close friends and family around you will help when you are feeling at your weakest and most vulnerable.

Any loss can be the cause of grief.
Grief doesn't have to just come from losing a loved one or pet. It could be from losing a job, a house, a particular time in your life. You can even have grief from positive changes like getting sober, leaving an abusive relationship, or giving birth. You don't have to feel unjustified, guilty, or silly for grieving over anything.

Accept and experience your feelings.

It can be tempting to try to numb your feelings with drugs or alcohol after a loss. This can include distracting yourself from the loss with work, staying busy all the time, bingeing Netflix, or playing a lot of video games. Sitting with and feeling painful emotions can be awful. However, if we ignore them long enough, they can manifest in health issues such as chronic pain, depression, or anxiety. Mindfulness practices such as the ones I outline in this book can help you recognize your feelings and accept them without judging yourself.

Grow from the loss.

If a loss seems meaningless, then it will be much harder to get over. Reframing the loss can help. For example, you can re-evaluate what you care about in life and make changes that you wouldn't have otherwise.

Grief isn't a problem to be solved, so don't try to.

Loss is a natural part of life and will happen to everyone eventually. It is easy to view it as a bad thing and something we want to avoid, but it is as natural as breathing. It's something we have to live through in our own time. It's okay to not be okay.

if you are
FEELING EFFECTS OF TRAUMA OR PTSD

Most people, at some point in their lives, have gone through traumatic experiences. We don't have to have a history of sexual or physical abuse to suffer from the effects of trauma, and PTSD isn't just for people who have been to war. We all develop unique defense mechanisms in childhood that we use to cope with the world. Sometimes these coping skills are no longer useful to us and can cause problems later in life.

Notice the symptoms.

Some of you might be wondering what the symptoms of trauma/PTSD are. There can be a lot of them, but a few signs that you might have trauma are:

- Feeling really distressed when thinking about a tragic event.
- Physical reactions to reminders of the event such as flinching, sweating, or pounding heart.
- Invasive thoughts or flashbacks about the memory that can appear at inconvenient or random times.
- Difficulty remembering certain parts of a traumatic event.
- Tendency to "numb out" with addictive behaviors such as using drugs or drinking.
- Trouble sleeping.
- Other mental illnesses, such as depression, anxiety, and panic attacks.

If you are having flashbacks or intrusive thoughts about the event, notice how you are feeling at that particular moment. Do you start sweating? Do you feel a tight sensation in your chest or throat?

Don't blame yourself.

Many people who have been the victims of abuse or violence can often feel tempted to blame themselves for how they are acting now. It's important to remember that your trauma is not your fault, but feel empowered knowing that you can take steps to heal from it.

Identify triggers.

Take a note of whether certain activities, people, or places trigger your symptoms. For example, I experienced a physical shudder when changing lanes for over two years after I was in a bad car accident. It's often not practical to avoid these triggers, but can help your therapist identify what you need to work on.

Get EMDR or Cognitive Behavior Therapy (CBT) to help process through the traumatic event.

Trauma results from the brain not being able to process that an event happened in the past. Instead, the sufferer is forced to re-experience the event over and over through flashbacks or intrusive memories. EMDR stands for "eye movement desensitization and reprocessing" and is a newer method of psychiatry that has proven incredibly successful in helping people recover from PTSD and traumatic experiences. How it basically works is that your therapist will have you talk through the traumatic incident. While you are talking, they will begin moving their finger back and forth, instructing you to follow with your eyes. The movement triggers the left and right sides of our brain, allowing new neural pathways to form. It is not known precisely how EMDR works, but has shown a success rate of about 80 percent when it comes to PTSD. Cognitive Behavioral Therapy has also been shown to help people who have experienced trauma.

if you are
⚡FEELING MANIC⚡

If you have been diagnosed with Bipolar Disorder 1 or 2, you might have experienced manic episodes. Symptoms of mania can include:

- Feelings of inflated self-esteem and importance.
- Lack of sleep.
- Inability to "read a room."
- Having racing thoughts.
- Engaging in risky and impulsive behaviors such as spending too much money or unusual sexual promiscuity.
- Becoming easily distracted.

If you are currently feeling manic, here are a few immediate and preventative steps you can take to help.

Reach out to your support team.

If you have a therapist or psychiatrist, call them and let them know you are having a manic episode. You can also ask a trusted friend or family member to help you through your manic time. This could mean making sure you don't engage in risky behaviors such as overspending.

Avoid triggering behaviors.
Manic episodes can be caused by a variety of factors, including drugs, alcohol, prescription drugs, or lack of sleep. If you are feeling manic, be sure to avoid drugs and alcohol and try your best to stick to a regular sleeping schedule.

Have a contingency plan set in place.
If you can start recognizing that you might be entering a manic episode, then you can plan for how to combat some of the adverse side effects. This may include making sure you can't access all of your money during this time, or ask a friend to check on you every day or so.

Make sure you don't forget to take your prescribed medication.
Sometimes manic behavior can cause one to forget that they need to take their medication or convince themselves that they don't actually need to take it. This can be incredibly dangerous as coming off mood-stabilizers can make manic and depressive symptoms worse. Set reminders for yourself to remember to take them. If you do ever decide you want to get off your medications, do not do it without the supervision of your doctor or psychiatrist.

if you are
FEELING LIKE YOU MIGHT RELAPSE

Remember, no matter what addiction you are recovering from, cravings are normal and can pop up at the least expected of times. When this happens, know that it is absolutely not your fault, and remember that having cravings does NOT mean you are weak.

Recognize the trigger.
What caused the craving? Are you in a situation where you used to use? Are you around old friends? Is today a significant date for you? Identify what might be making you have a craving and notice it without judgment. It's okay to have a craving, and know that you do not have to act on it.

Play out the situation in your mind.
Let's say you did use or self-harm. Play through the whole scenario. Maybe it is fun or feels good for a while. What happens after that? Do you wake up the next day feeling terrible? Do you do things that are dangerous or embarrassing? Do you have to lie to friends and family about your relapse? It's easy to think of the instant gratification you would get from a relapse, and forget how you would feel after.

Call your sponsor or support group.

If you think you are at immediate risk for a relapse, call your sponsor if you have one or talk to someone you trust. This will help distract you from the craving long enough that it may go away. Your sponsor will also be able to help with reminding you why you quit in the first place.

Write out a list of all the reasons why you wanted to quit your addictive behavior in the first place.

Sometimes it is easy to forget our reasons for quitting, and we want to give in to the temporary pleasure that comes from a relapse. If we can remember *why* we quit in the first place, it will help us to not want to repeat old habits. I've left some space down below to write some of those reasons. Take a couple of minutes to write as many as you can.

Why I quit:

How to do these journal exercises

Visual Mindfulness Exercises

This section will help you understand what is going on in the daily journaling pages, so don't skip it!

The first prompt on each of the journaling pages is to be mindful for a few minutes. I call this mindfulness because it's not a formal sitting meditation or anything like that. Basically, just sit with your thoughts for a couple of minutes before writing.

Notice if your mind is busy, or calm. Notice what thoughts are repeating. Maybe label the thoughts as "worrying," "planning," or "feeling." Focus on staying in the present moment. Typically, mindfulness exercises will have you notice your breath go in and out. I find this works, but I also like some sort of visual exercise to accompany the thought of my breath. On the next few pages are some visual mindfulness exercises that will help you stay present and notice your thoughts. Feel free to switch up which ones are most helpful to you.

Here are a few things you can visualize during your mindfulness session.

Leaf on a River

Visualize a little creek or stream. Give it a size, direction, and setting. As you think of the river, you will probably have other thoughts that appear. That's okay. For every thought that pops into your head, imagine putting it on a leaf. Then let that leaf flow down the river. Don't try to rush it away or force it to leave. Just watch it as it flows down the stream.

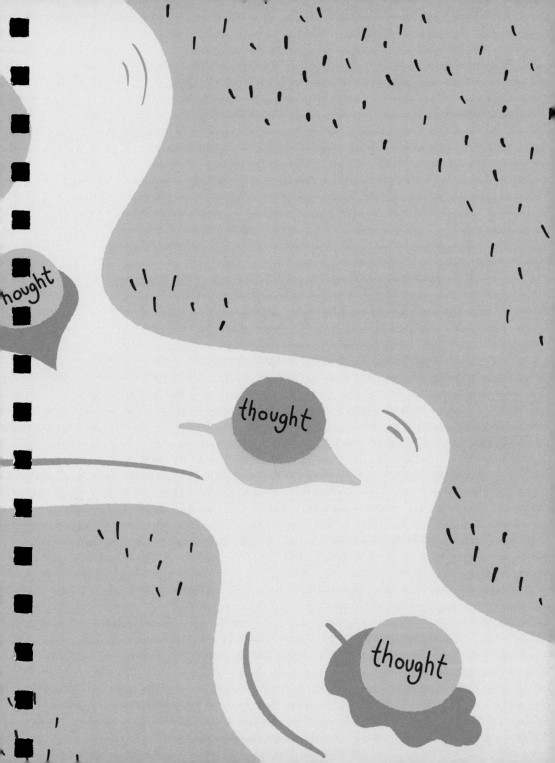

thought

thought

Clouds in the Sky

Visualize a big, open expanse of sky. It can be whatever time of day you want. As you stare up at the sky, you will most likely have thoughts that come visit you. Picture the thoughts sitting on clouds as they pass by. Each one should sit on its own cloud as they drift by. Remember, don't judge yourself for having the thoughts; just notice them with a faint sense of curiosity.

thought

thought

thought

thought

thought

Candle Breathing

This exercise will help you focus on your breathing. Close your eyes. Imagine a candle in front of you. What does the candle look like? Does it have a smell? How big is the flame? Now notice your breath coming in and out. As you breathe out, focus on how the light of the candle flickers with your exhalation. Focus on how your breathing affects the flame. If thoughts come to you, notice them, and then return your attention to the candle flame. Maybe you can put the thought in the flame and let it burn up and turn to ash.

Birds in the Park

Close your eyes. Imagine you are sitting on a park bench somewhere enjoying the feeling of your breath going in and out. Maybe there is a pile of seeds on the ground in front of you. As you sit, notice if thoughts come to you. If they do, imagine the thought like a bird pecking at the seeds. What does it look like? Is it a big crow? A small sparrow? Notice it visiting you on your park bench. Let it stay with you as long as you need, and then watch it as it flies off. Don't try to control the birds or shoo them away, just watch them calmly.

Perpetual Motion Machine

Sit with your eyes closed for a few minutes. In your brain, begin to imagine a simple machine. It can be anything—a motor, a set of gears, a series of pulleys, a top. I think of a bicycle chain and pedals, because it is a machine I am very familiar with. Imagine all the parts in as much detail as you can. Then let the device start working. For my bicycle machine, I watch the pedals move around, which runs the gear, which pulls the chain, which spins a wheel. Let it go as fast or as slow as you need it to go. If you get distracted, just notice that you are distracted and move your thoughts back to your perpetual motion machine.

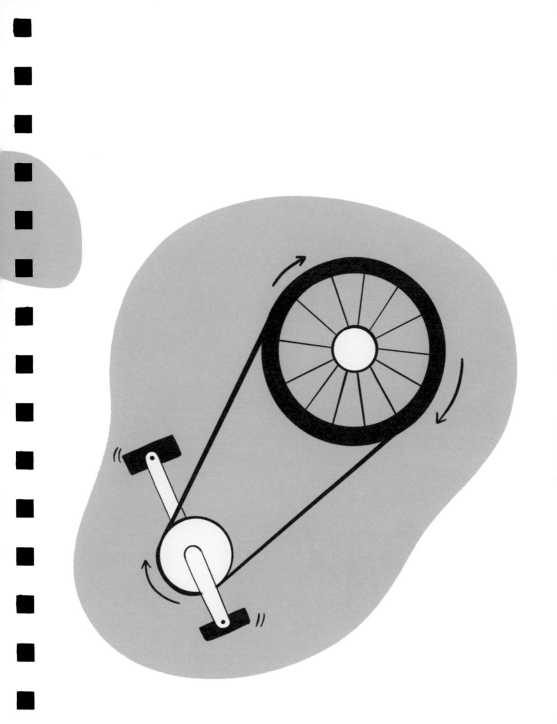

Visual Thought Recognition and Decoupling

After you sit with your thoughts in the mindfulness exercises, you may have noticed that some ideas stick around longer than others, or certain thoughts are more upsetting. The second part of the daily journal is to point out what thoughts you need help processing through. The first step is to write out a thought you noticed that isn't helpful to you anymore. It could be anything from *I'm a failure* to *If I don't do x, my entire life will end up in shambles*. As a practice run, write down a thought you have frequently that isn't helpful (even if you believe that it might be right).

A not-helpful thought:

The idea of this decoupling exercise is to recognize that your thoughts are not you, they are not necessarily true, and that they are just words. A lot of times, we hear our thoughts so clearly in our brains over and over again that we just automatically begin to accept what they say as truth. Here's the thing:

Our brain basically just farts out thoughts ALL THE TIME.

Let's do an experiment right now.

I want you to think really, really, really hard, *I can't move my toes.* Think it over and over for the next ten seconds. Now, while you are still thinking, I want you to move your toes. Did you wiggle them? Did it take you a second? Sometimes we get so invested in the story our brain is telling us that we believe even the silliest stories it tells. If you ever find yourself caught up in believing a story your mind is telling you, you can try the toe trick, or you can try a few of these other exercises.

Exercise 1

Take the not-helpful thought you wrote out earlier.
Below, write out all the letters in the silliest handwriting you can muster.

I'm not GOOD eNOUGH

Exercise 2

Write out the thought with the words out of order. Now write it again
but with all the letters out of order. Write it backward. Now upside-down.

Exercise 3

Look at the thought and say it in your head in a funny voice.
Imagine a cartoon character saying it. Fill it out in the chat bubble below.

See? Now the thought doesn't seem so big and scary, does it?

Dot Tracking Method

I came up with this goal tracking method a few years ago. It helps me put less pressure on myself while still helping me visualize my progress. I hate calendar-based goal tackers because any time I miss a day, it really demotivates me and gives me an excuse to give up. For example, I could say, "I missed my exercise goal today, so what's the point of working out tomorrow?" The dot-tracker eliminates the fear of missing a day.

Each day I meet my goal, I track it with a single dot.

Over time the dots build up, and you can see your small steps become something bigger, but you won't know how many days you missed. I typically use a fat marker to add more "oomph" to my dots. Stickers work great, too. We will practice using the dot tracker in the "Overall Intentions" section of the journal.

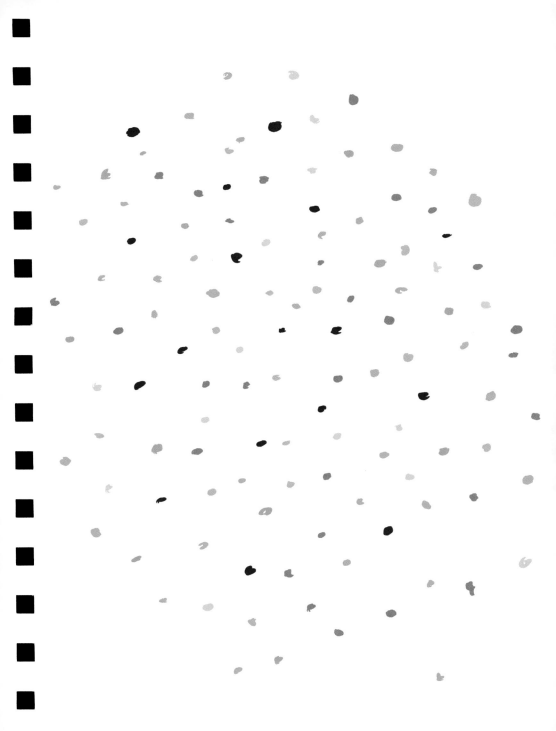

45

Visual Haiku

Don't worry. This isn't actually a complicated haiku with a certain number of syllables or anything. Basically, I try to take a core thought or feeling and break it down into something so simple that I can fit it all into a four-panel comic.

Here's how it works:
* Take the unhelpful thought you identified earlier. Now think about how you can simplify it, change it, or reverse it.
* Write out the thought, breaking it up in the four separate panels on the next page.
* Can you think of anything visual that might go along with each panel? If something comes to you, you can add a small drawing in each panel. If you like the way the words look, you can just leave it the way it is.
* You're done! Now you've broken up the thought and given it some space. Your very own Visual Haiku!

Sharing
One of the biggest helps to me getting through my depression and alcohol addiction was sharing my journey with others. When I quit drinking for good, I decided I wanted to make a comic every day of my sobriety for the first month and share it on Instagram. Feel free to share your visual haikus with your friends or on social media. You might find a lot of people can relate to what you are thinking or feeling.

47

Finding Your "Why"

Fill out this page before going to the daily journal pages. This is a good reference point that you can come back to when you are feeling lost or confused or don't know what to do on the journal page.

Setting your intentions/values

First things first, we need to figure out WHY you care about finishing this journal or working on yourself in the first place. To do this, we need to find out what your values are and then see how this journal fits in with them. Values are traits that you want to live by and are better than short-term goals because they can be worked on every single day and are never complete. For example, something I value is being creative. This is different than setting a judgmental goal. An example of a judgmental goal would be, "I want to be a successful artist." By saying "successful," we limit our satisfaction in life to an impossible-to-define standard. If I live by my value of being creative, then I have succeeded any time I paint or draw or write.

Once we know what our values are, we can become better at recognizing how we are living by our values, even if we don't reach our goals. For example, living by my artistic values might mean I enter a painting into a gallery. Even if it gets rejected, I can still view the painting as a success because I was practicing my value of being creative.

Let's help you determine what your values are!

On the next page is a list of common values to help get you started. You can choose from these or add in your own. Be sure to write or circle every single thing that you would consider one of your values in life.

honesty Curiosity INTEGRITY

BRAVERY SUSTAINABILITY

BEING OUTSIDE IN NATURE

RESPONSIBILITY

taking care of my family kindness

EMPATHY Gratitude Honor

being loving exploration

GROWTH learning TRUTH Passion

forgiveness

COURAGE taking care of my body

CREATIVITY

PATIENCE Respect

49

MY VALUES

Okay, once you've written down everything or circled the values you like, try to narrow it down to your five or six most important values. Once you have narrowed it down, write them out on the next page. Feel free to get colorful or creative on this page, so you can have a visual picture in your mind of what your core values are. Have fun with it and maybe even take a picture and set it as your phone background to help you remember. Now think about how this journal fits into your values and go forward knowing that you are on the first step to living by them!

Values Dot Tracker

Now that you have your values and figured out how this journal fits in with them, we can practice using the dot tracking method. On the next page is the Values Dot Tracker. Every time you live by your values, you can come here to add a dot. You can use each daily dot tracker to help remind you how many dots to add, or you can just guesstimate. This tracker is for you and you alone, so don't worry about being super accurate.

On the next page, write out your five or six values that you identified for reference and mark one dot for reading this part of the journal. Congrats! You are on your way to living the way you want to.

My Values

Track your dots here

PAGES

DATE:

Go through a visual mindfulness exercise for a couple minutes.
Today, try the "Candle Breathing" exercise. How was it?

Was your mind wandering or telling you old unhelpful stories? Write out what
your mind was thinking about below. Notice any helpful or unhelpful thoughts.

Mark a dot for every time you
stuck by your values today!

Brain Dump:

Create a visual haiku about what you were thinking about today.

Was it a good one? Share it!

DATE:

Go through a visual mindfulness exercise for a couple minutes.
Today, try the "Birds in the Park" exercise. How was it?

Was your mind wandering or telling you old unhelpful stories? Write out what
your mind was thinking about below. Notice any helpful or unhelpful thoughts.

Mark a dot for every time you
stuck by your values today!

Brain Dump:

Create a visual haiku about what you were thinking about today.

Excellent work!

DATE:

Go through a visual mindfulness exercise for a couple minutes. Today, try the "Perpetual Motion Machine" exercise. How was it?

Was your mind wandering or telling you old unhelpful stories? Write out what your mind was thinking about below. Notice any helpful or unhelpful thoughts.

Mark a dot for every time you stuck by your values today!

Brain Dump:

Create a visual haiku about what you were thinking about today.

You got this!

DATE:

Go through a visual mindfulness exercise for a couple minutes.
Today, try the "Clouds in the Sky" exercise. How was it?

Was your mind wandering or telling you old unhelpful stories? Write out what
your mind was thinking about below. Notice any helpful or unhelpful thoughts.

Mark a dot for every time you
stuck by your values today!

Brain Dump:

Create a visual haiku about what you were thinking about today.

Share your haiku with someone!

DATE:

Go through a visual mindfulness exercise for a couple minutes.
Today, try the "Leaf on a River" exercise. How was it?

Was your mind wandering or telling you old unhelpful stories? Write out what
your mind was thinking about below. Notice any helpful or unhelpful thoughts.

Mark a dot for every time you
stuck by your values today!

Brain Dump:

Create a visual haiku about what you were thinking about today.

Hope you are doing well!

DATE:

Go through a visual mindfulness exercise for a couple minutes.
Today, try the "Candle Breathing" exercise. How was it?

Was your mind wandering or telling you old unhelpful stories? Write out what
your mind was thinking about below. Notice any helpful or unhelpful thoughts.

Mark a dot for every time you
stuck by your values today!

Brain Dump:

Create a visual haiku about what you were thinking about today.

Thanks for taking care of yourself!

DATE:

Go through a visual mindfulness exercise for a couple minutes.
Today, try the "Birds in the Park" exercise. How was it?

Was your mind wandering or telling you old unhelpful stories? Write out what
your mind was thinking about below. Notice any helpful or unhelpful thoughts.

Mark a dot for every time you
stuck by your values today!

Brain Dump:

Create a visual haiku about what you were thinking about today.

Now that feels better!

DATE:

Go through a visual mindfulness exercise for a couple minutes.
Today, try the "Perpetual Motion Machine" exercise. How was it?

Was your mind wandering or telling you old unhelpful stories? Write out what
your mind was thinking about below. Notice any helpful or unhelpful thoughts.

Mark a dot for every time you
stuck by your values today!

Brain Dump:

Create a visual haiku about what you were thinking about today.

Keep growing!

DATE:

Go through a visual mindfulness exercise for a couple minutes.
Today, try the "Clouds in the Sky" exercise. How was it?

Was your mind wandering or telling you old unhelpful stories? Write out what
your mind was thinking about below. Notice any helpful or unhelpful thoughts.

Mark a dot for every time you
stuck by your values today!

Brain Dump:

Create a visual haiku about what you were thinking about today.

Draw your heart out!

DATE:

Go through a visual mindfulness exercise for a couple minutes.
Today, try the "Leaf on a River" exercise. How was it?

Was your mind wandering or telling you old unhelpful stories? Write out what
your mind was thinking about below. Notice any helpful or unhelpful thoughts.

Mark a dot for every time you
stuck by your values today!

Brain Dump:

Create a visual haiku about what you were thinking about today.

You're killing it!

DATE:

Go through a visual mindfulness exercise for a couple minutes.
Today, try the "Candle Breathing" exercise. How was it?

Was your mind wandering or telling you old unhelpful stories? Write out what
your mind was thinking about below. Notice any helpful or unhelpful thoughts.

Mark a dot for every time you
stuck by your values today!

Brain Dump:

Create a visual haiku about what you were thinking about today.

Was it a good one? Share it!

DATE:

Go through a visual mindfulness exercise for a couple minutes.
Today, try the "Birds in the Park" exercise. How was it?

Was your mind wandering or telling you old unhelpful stories? Write out what
your mind was thinking about below. Notice any helpful or unhelpful thoughts.

Mark a dot for every time you
stuck by your values today!

Brain Dump:

Create a visual haiku about what you were thinking about today.

Excellent work!

DATE:

Go through a visual mindfulness exercise for a couple minutes.
Today, try the "Perpetual Motion Machine" exercise. How was it?

Was your mind wandering or telling you old unhelpful stories? Write out what
your mind was thinking about below. Notice any helpful or unhelpful thoughts.

Mark a dot for every time you
stuck by your values today!

Brain Dump:

Create a visual haiku about what you were thinking about today.

You got this!

DATE:

Go through a visual mindfulness exercise for a couple minutes.
Today, try the "Clouds in the Sky" exercise. How was it?

Was your mind wandering or telling you old unhelpful stories? Write out what
your mind was thinking about below. Notice any helpful or unhelpful thoughts.

Mark a dot for every time you
stuck by your values today!

Brain Dump:

Create a visual haiku about what you were thinking about today.

Share your haiku with someone!

DATE:

Go through a visual mindfulness exercise for a couple minutes.
Today, try the "Leaf on a River" exercise. How was it?

Was your mind wandering or telling you old unhelpful stories? Write out what
your mind was thinking about below. Notice any helpful or unhelpful thoughts.

Mark a dot for every time you
stuck by your values today!

Brain Dump:

Create a visual haiku about what you were thinking about today.

Hope you are doing well!

DATE:

Go through a visual mindfulness exercise for a couple minutes.
Today, try the "Candle Breathing" exercise. How was it?

Was your mind wandering or telling you old unhelpful stories? Write out what
your mind was thinking about below. Notice any helpful or unhelpful thoughts.

Mark a dot for every time you
stuck by your values today!

Brain Dump:

Create a visual haiku about what you were thinking about today.

Thanks for taking care of yourself!

DATE:

Go through a visual mindfulness exercise for a couple minutes.
Today, try the "Birds in the Park" exercise. How was it?

Was your mind wandering or telling you old unhelpful stories? Write out what
your mind was thinking about below. Notice any helpful or unhelpful thoughts.

Mark a dot for every time you
stuck by your values today!

Brain Dump:

Create a visual haiku about what you were thinking about today.

Now that feels better!

DATE:

Go through a visual mindfulness exercise for a couple minutes.
Today, try the "Perpetual Motion Machine" exercise. How was it?

Was your mind wandering or telling you old unhelpful stories? Write out what
your mind was thinking about below. Notice any helpful or unhelpful thoughts.

Mark a dot for every time you
stuck by your values today!

Brain Dump:

Create a visual haiku about what you were thinking about today.

Keep growing!

DATE:

Go through a visual mindfulness exercise for a couple minutes.
Today, try the "Clouds in the Sky" exercise. How was it?

Was your mind wandering or telling you old unhelpful stories? Write out what
your mind was thinking about below. Notice any helpful or unhelpful thoughts.

Mark a dot for every time you
stuck by your values today!

Brain Dump:

Create a visual haiku about what you were thinking about today.

Draw your heart out!

DATE:

Go through a visual mindfulness exercise for a couple minutes.
Today, try the "Leaf on a River" exercise. How was it?

Was your mind wandering or telling you old unhelpful stories? Write out what
your mind was thinking about below. Notice any helpful or unhelpful thoughts.

Mark a dot for every time you
stuck by your values today!

Brain Dump:

Create a visual haiku about what you were thinking about today.

You're killing it!

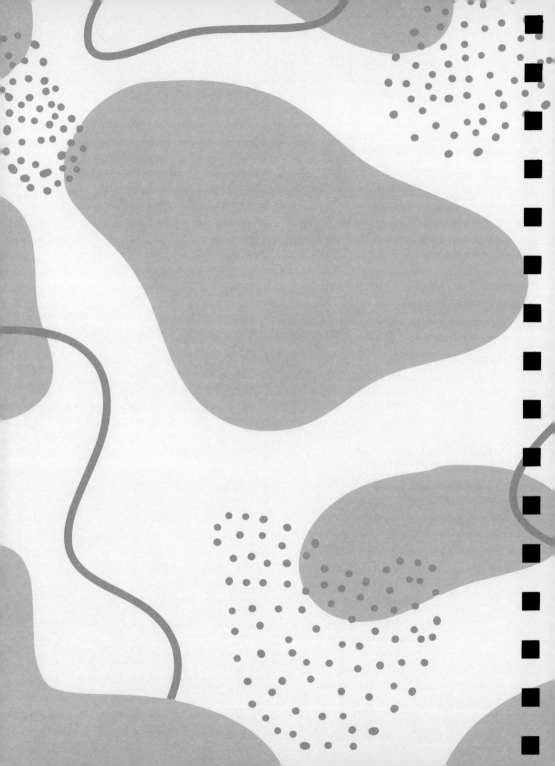

DATE:

Go through a visual mindfulness exercise for a couple minutes.
Today, try the "Candle Breathing" exercise. How was it?

Was your mind wandering or telling you old unhelpful stories? Write out what
your mind was thinking about below. Notice any helpful or unhelpful thoughts.

Mark a dot for every time you
stuck by your values today!

Brain Dump:

Create a visual haiku about what you were thinking about today.

Was it a good one? Share it!

DATE:

Go through a visual mindfulness exercise for a couple minutes.
Today, try the "Birds in the Park" exercise. How was it?

Was your mind wandering or telling you old unhelpful stories? Write out what
your mind was thinking about below. Notice any helpful or unhelpful thoughts.

Mark a dot for every time you
stuck by your values today!

Brain Dump:

Create a visual haiku about what you were thinking about today.

Excellent work!

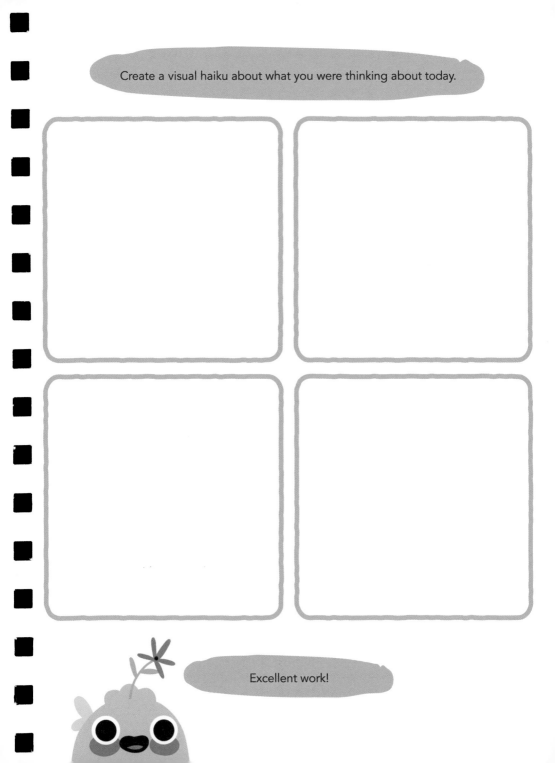

DATE:

Go through a visual mindfulness exercise for a couple minutes.
Today, try the "Perpetual Motion Machine" exercise. How was it?

Was your mind wandering or telling you old unhelpful stories? Write out what
your mind was thinking about below. Notice any helpful or unhelpful thoughts.

Mark a dot for every time you
stuck by your values today!

Brain Dump:

Create a visual haiku about what you were thinking about today.

You got this!

DATE:

Go through a visual mindfulness exercise for a couple minutes.
Today, try the "Clouds in the Sky" exercise. How was it?

Was your mind wandering or telling you old unhelpful stories? Write out what
your mind was thinking about below. Notice any helpful or unhelpful thoughts.

Mark a dot for every time you
stuck by your values today!

Brain Dump:

Create a visual haiku about what you were thinking about today.

Share your haiku with someone!

DATE:

Go through a visual mindfulness exercise for a couple minutes.
Today, try the "Leaf on a River" exercise. How was it?

Was your mind wandering or telling you old unhelpful stories? Write out what
your mind was thinking about below. Notice any helpful or unhelpful thoughts.

Mark a dot for every time you
stuck by your values today!

Brain Dump:

Create a visual haiku about what you were thinking about today.

Hope you are doing well!

DATE:

Go through a visual mindfulness exercise for a couple minutes.
Today, try the "Candle Breathing" exercise. How was it?

Was your mind wandering or telling you old unhelpful stories? Write out what
your mind was thinking about below. Notice any helpful or unhelpful thoughts.

Mark a dot for every time you
stuck by your values today!

Brain Dump:

Create a visual haiku about what you were thinking about today.

Thanks for taking care of yourself!

DATE:

Go through a visual mindfulness exercise for a couple minutes.
Today, try the "Birds in the Park" exercise. How was it?

Was your mind wandering or telling you old unhelpful stories? Write out what
your mind was thinking about below. Notice any helpful or unhelpful thoughts.

Mark a dot for every time you
stuck by your values today!

Brain Dump:

Create a visual haiku about what you were thinking about today.

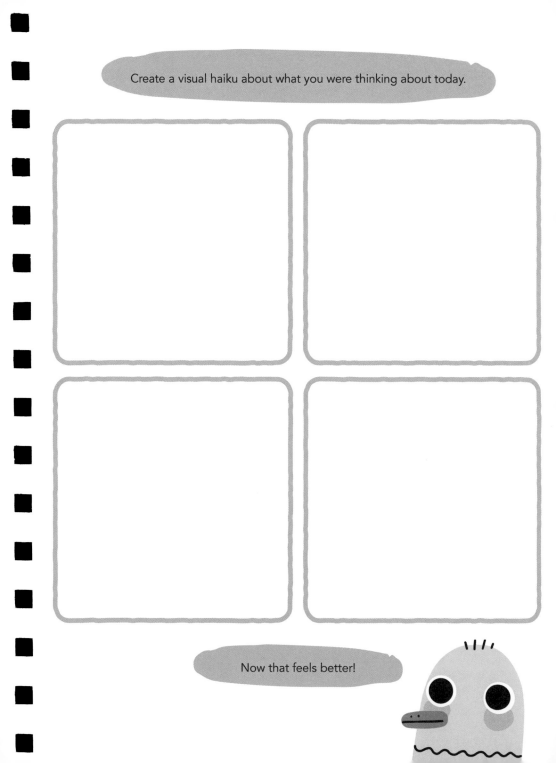

Now that feels better!

DATE:

Go through a visual mindfulness exercise for a couple minutes. Today, try the "Perpetual Motion Machine" exercise. How was it?

Was your mind wandering or telling you old unhelpful stories? Write out what your mind was thinking about below. Notice any helpful or unhelpful thoughts.

Mark a dot for every time you stuck by your values today!

Brain Dump:

Create a visual haiku about what you were thinking about today.

Keep growing!

DATE:

Go through a visual mindfulness exercise for a couple minutes.
Today, try the "Clouds in the Sky" exercise. How was it?

Was your mind wandering or telling you old unhelpful stories? Write out what
your mind was thinking about below. Notice any helpful or unhelpful thoughts.

Mark a dot for every time you
stuck by your values today!

Brain Dump:

Create a visual haiku about what you were thinking about today.

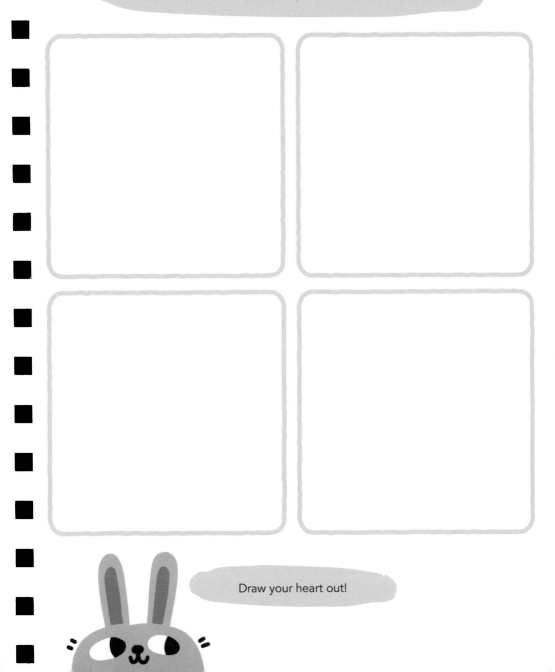

Draw your heart out!

DATE:

Go through a visual mindfulness exercise for a couple minutes.
Today, try the "Leaf on a River" exercise. How was it?

Was your mind wandering or telling you old unhelpful stories? Write out what
your mind was thinking about below. Notice any helpful or unhelpful thoughts.

Mark a dot for every time you
stuck by your values today!

Brain Dump:

Create a visual haiku about what you were thinking about today.

You're killing it!

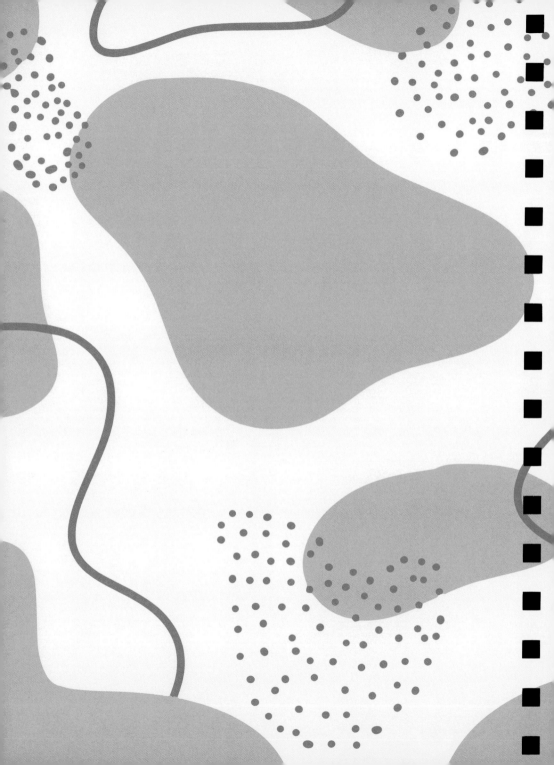

DATE:

Go through a visual mindfulness exercise for a couple minutes.
Today, try the "Candle Breathing" exercise. How was it?

Was your mind wandering or telling you old unhelpful stories? Write out what
your mind was thinking about below. Notice any helpful or unhelpful thoughts.

Mark a dot for every time you
stuck by your values today!

Brain Dump:

Create a visual haiku about what you were thinking about today.

Was it a good one? Share it!

DATE:

Go through a visual mindfulness exercise for a couple minutes.
Today, try the "Birds in the Park" exercise. How was it?

Was your mind wandering or telling you old unhelpful stories? Write out what
your mind was thinking about below. Notice any helpful or unhelpful thoughts.

Mark a dot for every time you
stuck by your values today!

Brain Dump:

Create a visual haiku about what you were thinking about today.

Excellent work!

DATE:

Go through a visual mindfulness exercise for a couple minutes.
Today, try the "Perpetual Motion Machine" exercise. How was it?

Was your mind wandering or telling you old unhelpful stories? Write out what
your mind was thinking about below. Notice any helpful or unhelpful thoughts.

Mark a dot for every time you
stuck by your values today!

Brain Dump:

Create a visual haiku about what you were thinking about today.

You got this!

DATE:

Go through a visual mindfulness exercise for a couple minutes.
Today, try the "Clouds in the Sky" exercise. How was it?

Was your mind wandering or telling you old unhelpful stories? Write out what
your mind was thinking about below. Notice any helpful or unhelpful thoughts.

Mark a dot for every time you
stuck by your values today!

Brain Dump:

Create a visual haiku about what you were thinking about today.

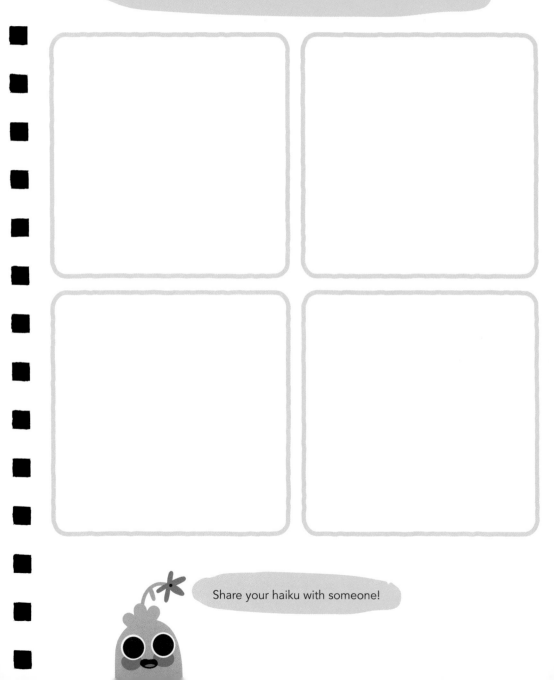

Share your haiku with someone!

DATE:

Go through a visual mindfulness exercise for a couple minutes.
Today, try the "Leaf on a River" exercise. How was it?

Was your mind wandering or telling you old unhelpful stories? Write out what
your mind was thinking about below. Notice any helpful or unhelpful thoughts.

Mark a dot for every time you
stuck by your values today!

Brain Dump:

Create a visual haiku about what you were thinking about today.

Hope you are doing well!

DATE:

Go through a visual mindfulness exercise for a couple minutes.
Today, try the "Candle Breathing" exercise. How was it?

Was your mind wandering or telling you old unhelpful stories? Write out what
your mind was thinking about below. Notice any helpful or unhelpful thoughts.

Mark a dot for every time you
stuck by your values today!

Brain Dump:

Create a visual haiku about what you were thinking about today.

Thanks for taking care of yourself!

DATE:

Go through a visual mindfulness exercise for a couple minutes.
Today, try the "Birds in the Park" exercise. How was it?

Was your mind wandering or telling you old unhelpful stories? Write out what
your mind was thinking about below. Notice any helpful or unhelpful thoughts.

Mark a dot for every time you
stuck by your values today!

Brain Dump:

Create a visual haiku about what you were thinking about today.

Now that feels better!

DATE:

Go through a visual mindfulness exercise for a couple minutes.
Today, try the "Perpetual Motion Machine" exercise. How was it?

Was your mind wandering or telling you old unhelpful stories? Write out what
your mind was thinking about below. Notice any helpful or unhelpful thoughts.

Mark a dot for every time you
stuck by your values today!

Brain Dump:

Create a visual haiku about what you were thinking about today.

Keep growing!

DATE:

Go through a visual mindfulness exercise for a couple minutes.
Today, try the "Clouds in the Sky" exercise. How was it?

Was your mind wandering or telling you old unhelpful stories? Write out what
your mind was thinking about below. Notice any helpful or unhelpful thoughts.

Mark a dot for every time you
stuck by your values today!

Brain Dump:

Create a visual haiku about what you were thinking about today.

Draw your heart out!

DATE:

Go through a visual mindfulness exercise for a couple minutes.
Today, try the "Leaf on a River" exercise. How was it?

Was your mind wandering or telling you old unhelpful stories? Write out what
your mind was thinking about below. Notice any helpful or unhelpful thoughts.

Mark a dot for every time you
stuck by your values today!

Brain Dump:

Create a visual haiku about what you were thinking about today.

You're killing it!

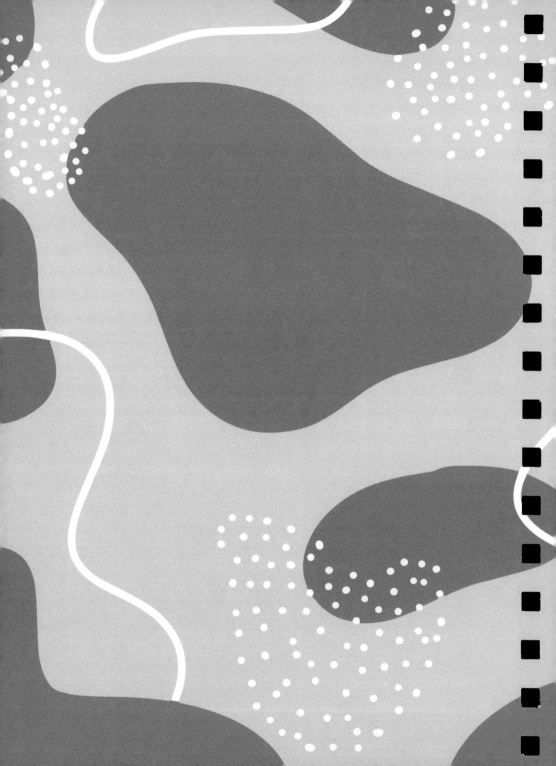

DATE:

Go through a visual mindfulness exercise for a couple minutes.
Today, try the "Candle Breathing" exercise. How was it?

Was your mind wandering or telling you old unhelpful stories? Write out what
your mind was thinking about below. Notice any helpful or unhelpful thoughts.

Mark a dot for every time you
stuck by your values today!

Brain Dump:

Create a visual haiku about what you were thinking about today.

Was it a good one? Share it!

DATE:

Go through a visual mindfulness exercise for a couple minutes.
Today, try the "Birds in the Park" exercise. How was it?

Was your mind wandering or telling you old unhelpful stories? Write out what
your mind was thinking about below. Notice any helpful or unhelpful thoughts.

Mark a dot for every time you
stuck by your values today!

Brain Dump:

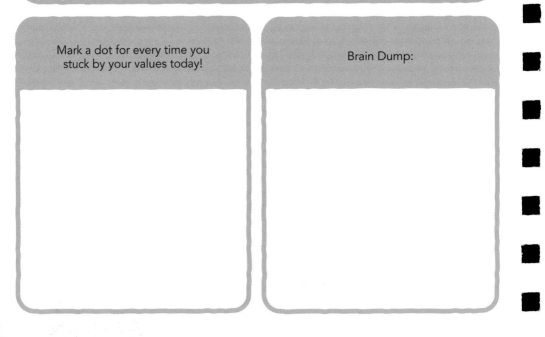

Create a visual haiku about what you were thinking about today.

Excellent work!

DATE:

Go through a visual mindfulness exercise for a couple minutes. Today, try the "Perpetual Motion Machine" exercise. How was it?

Was your mind wandering or telling you old unhelpful stories? Write out what your mind was thinking about below. Notice any helpful or unhelpful thoughts.

Mark a dot for every time you stuck by your values today!

Brain Dump:

Create a visual haiku about what you were thinking about today.

You got this!

DATE:

Go through a visual mindfulness exercise for a couple minutes.
Today, try the "Clouds in the Sky" exercise. How was it?

Was your mind wandering or telling you old unhelpful stories? Write out what
your mind was thinking about below. Notice any helpful or unhelpful thoughts.

Mark a dot for every time you
stuck by your values today!

Brain Dump:

Create a visual haiku about what you were thinking about today.

Share your haiku with someone!

DATE:

Go through a visual mindfulness exercise for a couple minutes.
Today, try the "Leaf on a River" exercise. How was it?

Was your mind wandering or telling you old unhelpful stories? Write out what
your mind was thinking about below. Notice any helpful or unhelpful thoughts.

Mark a dot for every time you
stuck by your values today!

Brain Dump:

Create a visual haiku about what you were thinking about today.

Hope you are doing well!

DATE:

Go through a visual mindfulness exercise for a couple minutes.
Today, try the "Candle Breathing" exercise. How was it?

Was your mind wandering or telling you old unhelpful stories? Write out what
your mind was thinking about below. Notice any helpful or unhelpful thoughts.

Mark a dot for every time you
stuck by your values today!

Brain Dump:

Create a visual haiku about what you were thinking about today.

Thanks for taking care of yourself!

DATE:

Go through a visual mindfulness exercise for a couple minutes.
Today, try the "Birds in the Park" exercise. How was it?

Was your mind wandering or telling you old unhelpful stories? Write out what
your mind was thinking about below. Notice any helpful or unhelpful thoughts.

Mark a dot for every time you
stuck by your values today!

Brain Dump:

Create a visual haiku about what you were thinking about today.

Now that feels better!

DATE:

Go through a visual mindfulness exercise for a couple minutes.
Today, try the "Perpetual Motion Machine" exercise. How was it?

Was your mind wandering or telling you old unhelpful stories? Write out what
your mind was thinking about below. Notice any helpful or unhelpful thoughts.

Mark a dot for every time you
stuck by your values today!

Brain Dump:

Create a visual haiku about what you were thinking about today.

Keep growing!

DATE:

Go through a visual mindfulness exercise for a couple minutes.
Today, try the "Clouds in the Sky" exercise. How was it?

Was your mind wandering or telling you old unhelpful stories? Write out what
your mind was thinking about below. Notice any helpful or unhelpful thoughts.

Mark a dot for every time you
stuck by your values today!

Brain Dump:

Create a visual haiku about what you were thinking about today.

Draw your heart out!

DATE:

Go through a visual mindfulness exercise for a couple minutes.
Today, try the "Leaf on a River" exercise. How was it?

Was your mind wandering or telling you old unhelpful stories? Write out what
your mind was thinking about below. Notice any helpful or unhelpful thoughts.

Mark a dot for every time you
stuck by your values today!

Brain Dump:

Create a visual haiku about what you were thinking about today.

You're killing it!

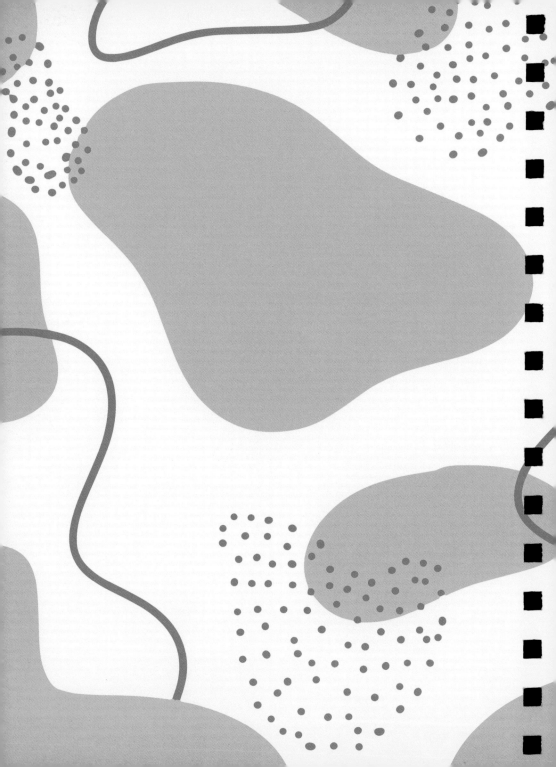

Resources

Online therapy, psychiatry & resources

American Foundation for Suicide Prevention
Afsp.org

Better Help Online Therapy
Betterhelp.com

Find a therapist in your area
Psychologytoday.com

More information about EMDR therapy
Emdr.com

Talkspace Online Therapy
Talkspace.com

A fun interactive website for when you are feeling like shit.
youfeellikeshit.com

Useful Apps

Calm—meditation app

Headspace—meditation app

I am Sober—addiction tracking app

Oak—meditation app

Presently—gratitude app

Procreate—how I draw all my comics

Shine—daily motivation app

TooBee—mindfulness reminder

Youtube—for learning, meditations, sleep aid videos

Podcasts

10% Happier Podcast—meditation for fidgety skeptics with Dan Harris

The Hilarious World of Depression—conversations with comedians who have depression

Sleep With Me—helps the listener fall asleep quickly

Books that have helped me

The Four Agreements: A Practical Guide to Personal Freedom by Don Miguel Ruiz

The Upward Spiral: Using Neuroscience to Reverse the Course of Depression, One Small Change at a Time by Alex Korb

This Naked Mind: Control Alcohol: Find Freedom, Rediscover Happiness & Change Your Life by Annie Grace

The Easy Way to Control Alcohol by Allen Carr

Radical Acceptance by Tara Brach

The Confidence Gap by Russ Harris

The Body Keeps the Score: Brain, Mind, and Body in the Healing of Trauma Book by Bessel van der Kolk

The Power of Now: A Guide to Spiritual Enlightenment by Eckhart Tolle

Addiction Recovery Groups/Training

Smart Recovery—In-person meetings that use CBT and other science-based methods of recovery.
Smartrecovery.org

Alcoholics Anonymous—In-person meetings that use the 12-step method of recovery.
aa.org

The Temper—online recovery program
jointempest.com

Allen Carr—online recovery programs
allencarr.com

Sharing the
AFSP Story

The American Foundation for Suicide Prevention (AFSP) is a voluntary health organization that gives those affected by suicide a nationwide community empowered by research, education, and advocacy to take action against this leading cause of death.

It is the mission of the AFSP to save lives and bring hope to those affected by suicide, which is one of the ten leading causes of death in the United States—and it's preventable. As these rates continue to rise, we must make mental health a national priority, and advocate for more investment in suicide research and nationwide prevention efforts. We must have real, honest conversations, and create a culture that's smart about mental health.

The **American Foundation for Suicide Prevention** is dedicated to saving lives and bringing hope to those affected by suicide. AFSP creates a culture that's smart about mental health through education and community programs, develops suicide prevention through research and advocacy, and provides support for those affected by suicide. Led by CEO Robert Gebbia and headquartered in New York with a public policy office in Washington, D.C., AFSP has local chapters in all 50 states with programs and events nationwide. Learn more about AFSP in its latest Annual Report, and join the conversation on suicide prevention by following AFSP on Facebook, Twitter, Instagram, and YouTube.

American Foundation *for* **Suicide Prevention**

About the Artist

Holly Chisholm

Holly Chisholm is the creator of the Just Peachy Comic series and author of *Just Peachy: Comics about Depression, Anxiety, Love, and Finding the Humor in Being Sad*, and a mental health and addiction recovery advocate. She lives in Mesa, Arizona, with her boyfriend, Matt; her dog, Bubbles; a hairless cat named Cosmo; and cranky cockatiel named Larry.

She had her last drink September 30, 2019.